MAR 2009

Justin Timberlake

Justin Timberlake

by Terri Dougherty

LUCENT BOOKS
A part of Gale, Cengage Learning

GALE
CENGAGE Learning™

Detroit • New York • San Francisco • New Haven, Conn • Waterville, Maine • London

GALE
CENGAGE Learning™

LIBRARY OF CONGRESS CATALOGING-IN-PUBLICATION DATA

Dougherty, Terri.
  Justin Timberlake / by Terri Dougherty.
    p. cm. — (People in the news)
  Includes bibliographical references and index.
  ISBN: 978-1-4205-0056-1 (hardcover)
    1. Timberlake, Justin, 1981—Juvenile literature. 2. Singers—United States—
Biography—Juvenile literature. I. Title.
  ML3930.T58D68 2008
  782.42164092—dc22
  [B]
                                                                              2008004172

Lucent Books
27500 Drake Rd
Farmington Hills MI 48331

ISBN-13: 978-1-4205-0056-1
ISBN-10: 1-4205-0056-2

Contents

Fame and celebrity are alluring. People are drawn to those who walk in fame's spotlight, whether they are known for great accomplishments or for notorious deeds. The lives of the famous pique public interest and attract attention, perhaps because their experiences seem in some ways so different from, yet in other ways so similar to, our own.

Newspapers, magazines, and television regularly capitalize on this fascination with celebrity by running profiles of famous people. For example, television programs such as *Entertainment Tonight* devote all their programming to stories about entertainment and entertainers. Magazines such as *People* fill their pages with stories of the private lives of famous people. Even newspapers, newsmagazines, and television news frequently delve into the lives of well-known personalities. Despite the number of articles and programs, few provide more than a superficial glimpse at their subjects.

Lucent's People in the News series offers young readers a deeper look into the lives of today's newsmakers, the influences that have shaped them, and the impact they have had in their fields of endeavor and on other people's lives. The subjects of the series hail from many disciplines and walks of life. They include authors, musicians, athletes, political leaders, entertainers, entrepreneurs, and others who have made a mark on modern life and who, in many cases, will continue to do so for years to come.

These biographies are more than factual chronicles. Each book emphasizes the contributions, accomplishments, or deeds that have brought fame or notoriety to the individual and shows how that person has influenced modern life. Authors portray their subjects in a realistic, unsentimental light. For example, Bill Gates —the cofounder and chief executive officer of the software giant Microsoft—has been instrumental in making personal computers the most vital tool of the modern age. Few dispute his business savvy, his perseverance, or his technical expertise, yet critics say he is ruthless in his dealings with competitors and driven more by his desire to maintain Microsoft's dominance in the computer industry than by an interest in furthering technology.

In these books, young readers will encounter inspiring stories about real people who achieved success despite enormous obstacles. Oprah Winfrey—the most powerful, most watched, and wealthiest woman on television today—spent the first six years of her life in the care of her grandparents while her unwed mother sought work and a better life elsewhere. Her adolescence was colored by promiscuity, pregnancy at age fourteen, rape, and sexual abuse.

Each author documents and supports his or her work with an array of primary and secondary source quotations taken from diaries, letters, speeches, and interviews. All quotes are footnoted to show readers exactly how and where biographers derive their information and provide guidance for further research. The quotations enliven the text by giving readers eyewitness views of the life and accomplishments of each person covered in the People in the News series.

In addition, each book in the series includes photographs, annotated bibliographies, timelines, and comprehensive indexes. For both the casual reader and the student researcher, the People in the News series offers insight into the lives of today's newsmakers—people who shape the way we live, work, and play in the modern age.

A Pop Star Grows Up

Justin Timberlake began his career as a Mouseketeer and grew up to become a rock star. After appearing on television as a child, he rose to teen pop stardom and then turned his attention to gaining respect as a musician. It was not an easy feat in a field where many pop stars fade into obscurity and many child entertainers struggle to continue their careers as adults. Timberlake beat the odds and found success.

Timberlake's accomplishments hinge on the fact that desire for popularity and fame has not been the driving force in his career. He does not want to be successful just for the sake of being a celebrity. He certainly enjoys the perks that come with being well known, but that is not why he pushes himself to succeed. Timberlake has found success because he loves performing and craves the respect of fellow musicians and entertainers, and to earn that respect he has not stopped learning and developing his talent.

To transition from a pop star in a boy band to a respected rocker and musician, Timberlake absorbed as much as he could from the people he has worked with. He began his career in the entertainment industry on the Disney Channel, as a member of the *Mickey Mouse Club*. His time on the show spanned only two years, but taught him a great deal about performing. Through the show he also made connections in the entertainment industry. He met people who helped keep his fledgling career from ending with the show.

Justin Timberlake (bottom right) rose to teen pop stardom as a member of the boy band *NSYNC.

After the *Mickey Mouse Club* ended, Timberlake became part of *NSYNC and finally a pop star. Timberlake rose to the forefront of the five-member group, with a tough guy image softened by a romantic relationship with pop star Britney Spears. It was a heady time for the young performer as he was adored by fans, sought after by the press, and featured on the cover of *Rolling Stone* magazine. He indulged in the celebrity lifestyle, with parties and fancy cars, but eventually began to look for more from his career than the trappings of fame.

Timberlake wanted more respect as a musician than being a member of a boy band could bring. He broke away from the commercial sound of pop music to see what kind of music he could create as a solo artist. He did not go it alone, however. Timberlake made connections in the music industry, and knew where to turn for help in changing his image.

For his first solo effort, *Justified*, Timberlake added hip-hop, funk, and rhythm and blues styles to his to music. He worked with producers such as Timbaland to create a distinctive sound, and the album earned him praise for his musical ability. He followed it with a second effort, *FutureSex/LoveSounds*, that brought accolades for his inspired songwriting. Timberlake's collaborations have been a success, as they have given him the unique sound he had been searching for and taught him even more about music. He lends his expertise to other artists as well, and has collaborated with performers from the hip-hop band Black Eyed Peas to country star Reba McEntire. The former *NSYNC lead singer has consistently surprised others with his innovative musical creations and impressed them with his abilities.

Timberlake's polished performances added to his reputation as a musician. Like one of his idols, singer Michael Jackson, Timberlake uses clever and energetic dance moves as well as vocal ability to impress audiences when he is performing. Drawing on his days as a member of *NSYNC, he concentrates on making his live shows entertainment packages, with lighting and video effects. Timberlake is a songwriter, producer, singer, and dancer who has taken chances with his career and as a result has grown as a performer.

Justin Timberlake (left) performing with his idol Michael Jackson. Like Jackson, Timberlake uses his vocal ability and dance moves to entertain audiences.

Timberlake has not limited his career to music, however. He has dabbled in acting as well and has shown natural comic timing with appearances on *Saturday Night Live*. Although he is more well known as a singer than an actor, trying something new gives him the opportunity to keep his work life interesting. Writing songs, creating an album, and touring to promote it are exhausting efforts that sap his creativity. To recharge, Timberlake takes time off and tries new things.

There is a commanding presence around Timberlake when he is onstage or onscreen, but he has a quiet and sensitive side as well. He prefers to keep his romantic relationships out of the public eye, taking care not to discuss them often in interviews. In addition, he remains close to his mother; she was the first one he called when he was the subject of a prank on the television show *Punk'd*.

Timberlake took the *Punk'd* joke in stride, but vowed to treat its producer, Ashton Kutcher, in kind. Timberlake did a parody of Kutcher and his show on *Saturday Night Live*. Timberlake is a person who accomplishes what he sets out to do and is not to be underestimated. The former boy band member proved this when he sought the respect that money could not buy. He earned it, doing something few expected from him when he hit the music scene as a member of *NSYNC as a teen-ager in the late 1990s. Since that time, the accomplished singer and performer has brought innovative sound and catchy lyrics to the radio airwaves, and has received praise from his fellow musicians along the way.

Chapter 1

This Kid Has Rhythm

Justin Timberlake's musical talent and knack for keeping a beat was apparent from the time he was a baby. Justin Randall Timberlake was born in Memphis, Tennessee, on January 31, 1981, to Lynn and Randy Timberlake. His hometown is a city of about 650,000 people in southwestern Tennessee overlooking the Mississippi River. It is one of the cities where blues-style music was developed and is also known for being the home of Graceland, the estate of singer Elvis Presley.

Music was big part of the Timberlake family's lifestyle. Randy Timberlake was in a bluegrass band, where he played bass and sang high harmonies. He also directed the choir in the Baptist church where Justin's grandfather was a minister. Justin's uncle, his mother's brother, was a musician as well, and was in the bluegrass band with Randy Timberlake.

It soon became evident that baby Justin had an innate feel for music. When he was only a few months old, his mom would put him in a little seat on the kitchen counter. Justin couldn't keep still and would move his legs to the beat of music he heard. "We'd change the music and he'd kick his legs to the new beat," his mom recalled. "We'd say to our friends, 'Dude! Look at this!' He was like a little toy."[1] By age two, he was singing the harmony parts to songs on the radio.

Life in the Timberlake household was not always harmonious. Lynn was only twenty years old when her son was born, and the

Family Ties

Although he began performing at a young age, Justin Timberlake always remained close to his family. He called his grandmother, Sadie Bomar, when he was coming home to Tennessee, telling her not to forget to make his peach cobbler. She even brought him a batch when he was touring with *NSYNC in 2000. He ate it on his tour bus and later was thoughtful enough to return her baking pan to her.

Timberlake is especially close to his mother. They grew up together, he said, and get along so well that it is difficult for other girls to measure up to her. "She's been my best friend since I figured out who I wanted to be," he said in 2003 to *Rolling Stone* writer Eric Hedegaard. "She's great and such a fun woman. She goes out with me and stays out later than I do. She's always been there beside me, and I think that's part of my problem with girls. You keep searching for somebody as good as your mother, and that's a losing battle."

Eric Hedegaard, "The Bachelor," *Rolling Stone*, January 23, 2003, p. 34.

marriage was shaky. She and Randy divorced when Timberlake was two.

Both parents remained close to Timberlake after the divorce, and he developed an especially strong bond with his mother. Lynn Timberlake remarried when Justin was five, becoming the wife of a banker named Paul Harless. Justin got along well with his stepfather. Justin's father also remarried and had two sons—Jonathan and Stephen—with his new wife.

Talented Youngster

Justin grew up in Millington, Tennessee, one of the main suburbs of Memphis. While he had a feel for music, as a young child he did not go out of his way to put on shows or entertain people

Because Justin's mom recognized that her son had an ability for singing at a young age she entered him into many talent shows.

around him. His mother described him as a quiet boy, who would walk around with his head down.

Music was all around Justin as he was growing up. He listened to country music on the radio and learned about singers such as Johnny Cash and Willie Nelson from his grandfather. He overcame his shyness to sing in the church gospel choir, and his grandfather also taught him the basics of playing guitar.

Justin's mom recognized his singing ability and thought her son had the potential to be a star. She encouraged her shy child to use his talent onstage. She entered him in talent shows, and he began performing under the name Justin Randall. He sang mainly country and gospel music because audiences seemed most interested in these music styles.

At age eight, Justin began taking voice lessons. His superior vocal talent and knack for performing soon became apparent to his classmates. When he was in third grade at E.E. Jeter Elementary School, he sang as the warm-up act for a lip-synching contest and impressed the audience. He was so good at the New Kids on the Block song he performed that girls mobbed him. "It was like something out of a Beatles movie," recalls Paul Harless, Justin's stepdad. "They had him pinned up against a wall. Some wanted to get his autograph. Some tried to give him money."[2]

Student of Music

The throng of adoring young fans did not scare Justin away from music or performing. The more he learned about music, the more intrigued he became. He spent his time learning about different styles and sounds and the layering of harmonies. At age eleven he was introduced to the blues and became interested in learning about its roots. In addition, he began to appreciate the rhythm and blues music of singers and musicians such as Al Green, Stevie Wonder, and Marvin Gaye.

His father's music collection also expanded his musical tastes. Randy Timberlake would play the Eagles and Bob Seger when Justin visited him. Justin also became interested in the harmonies of the rock group Queen, and was so taken by the song

Bohemian Rhapsody that he would lock himself in his room and listen carefully to the music and harmony, trying to learn every nuance.

Star Search

No longer shy about his vocal talent, Justin did not hesitate to show what he could do when his mom entered him in a number of talent shows. These shows allowed him to polish his singing talent and gain experience as a performer. Justin was learning to be comfortable onstage and impress an audience.

In 1992, at age eleven, he expanded his career beyond live talent shows and entered the realm of television with a tryout for the *Star Search* talent show. *Star Search* was a show on which contestants performed in front of a panel of judges for the chance to be on television and win a prize for their talent. Dressed in a cowboy hat and western shirt, Justin passed the audition and made it onto television as a contestant. However, the show's judges did not choose him as a winner when he performed on the show.

New Mouseketeer

The show helped the young performer attract notice, however, and expand his singing career. In 1993, he was selected to be part of *The Mickey Mouse Club* or *MMC*. He and his mother moved to Orlando, Florida, where the show was produced. The twelve-year-old left behind his home, friends, and ordinary life in Memphis for a chance to be part of a nationally televised show.

The Mickey Mouse Club was based on a similar series that was popular in the 1950s and had also been remade in the 1970s. The show brought together a number of talented young singers and dancers and had them perform songs, dances and short sketches. The show was packed with talent: Britney Spears, Christina Aguilera, and JC Chasez were all part of the show. Jessica Simpson tried out, but did not make the cut.

Justin's selection as a member of the show's cast changed his life. Until now, he had been an average student and a member

Many of the members of the cast of **The Mickey Mouse Club,** *like Justin (top right), used the show to jump start their television or singing careers.*

of the school's basketball team who spent some of his free time performing in talent shows. As a Mouseketeer, performing would be the main focus of his life.

Justin was on the show for almost two years. He spent a significant amount of time learning the songs, dance moves, and comedy sketches that were part of the show, but also enjoyed a number of perks as a cast member. He was now living close to Walt Disney World, and one of the things he loved doing was watching an attraction at Disney called the Captain EO show. The elaborate, 17-minute 3-D film starred Michael Jackson. The expensive movie was produced by *Star Wars* creator George Lucas and had a science fiction theme, with Jackson winning over an evil queen with music. Justin saw it more than twenty times, never tiring of Michael Jackson's musical ability.

Using his Talent

Justin had the opportunity to follow in the footsteps of his musical idol, Jackson, who had also begun his career as a young singer. *The Mickey Mouse Club* gave Justin a chance to learn more about singing and dancing and to perform what he learned onstage before a live audience. Justin began to appreciate what it was like to be in the spotlight. In one of the show's concert segments, Justin and Britney Spears did a duet of the song "I Feel For You," and even as a child Justin showed that he was a talented dancer and confident singer. He commanded attention onstage yet easily shared the spotlight with Spears.

Justin was not always the star of the show, however. He had his share of moments onstage, but also sang backup for the other performers. He learned how to perform as part of a group, not just as the center of attention.

In addition to song and dance routines, the show also featured profiles of the young actors in the cast. In his profile on *MMC*, he introduced kids to Memphis, the city where he grew up. He proudly showed off its trolleys, the amphitheater where he saw concerts, and Elvis's home at Graceland. It also showed his humorous side as he played golf and told kids that the key

In order to get his ear pierced Justin's stepfather made him sing "The Earring Song" to family and friends.

Earning His Earring

At age thirteen, Justin begged his parents to let him get his ear pierced. All his friends had earrings, he reasoned, and he should have one, too. His stepfather, Paul Harless, made Justin earn it rather than simply giving in to his request. If Justin would write a song and sing it at a family gathering, he could have his ear pierced, his stepfather said.

Justin really wanted that earring, so he wrote "The Earring Song" and sang it to his parents and a friend while they were on vacation in Hawaii. His stepfather kept his word. When they returned to Memphis, Justin got his earring.

---

to a good putt was to put the ball in the hole. The adventurous side of his personality was evident when he was shown riding a four-wheeler.

Justin stayed close to a number of his friends from Memphis even though he had moved to Orlando. He brought several of them onto the show with him for his profile segment. Viewers got a look into a natural and funny side of his personality as he and his friends did Elvis impersonations. Timberlake also toured the city with his friends, looking relaxed in front of the camera. It was not the city's attractions but its serenity that Justin said he liked.

Not All Easy

Justin had a group of close friends and a fun job as a performer, but he still had to deal with the problems faced by many young teens. Justin had acne and was called names such as "Pizza Face." His curly hair was difficult to manage. "I used to get picked on all the time," he said. "I had terrible acne, weird hair. My arms were too long."[3]

The Mickey Mouse Club was cancelled in 1995, and Disney stopped making new episodes. Justin was out of work but did not want to stop performing. The young singer looked for ways to keep his performing career alive. Fellow Mouseketeer JC Chasez shared Justin's interest. The pair went to Nashville to try to land a recording contract. They made a demo record, a recording they could send to record labels to show music industry executives their talent. They had little success until they received a call from Chris Kirkpatrick, another young singer and actor JC and Justin knew from auditions they had all attended at Disney and Universal Studios.

Forming *NSYNC

Chris called Justin and JC with the idea of forming a boy band. The pair saw this as a great way to continue their careers and agreed. The group needed a bass voice and found singer Joey Fatone. Although his voice was not low enough for a true bass, it blended well with the other boy's voices, and they decided to keep him in the group. Justin's vocal coach found the boys a fifth member, Lance Bass, who could hit the low notes.

*JC Chasez, Chris Kirkpatrick, and Justin Timberlake were the founding members of the boy band *NSYNC.*

The boy band was formed in 1995. Justin was one of the group's lead singers and was its youngest member. "We really put ourselves together," Justin said. "It's funny to look back on how we all came together; it just happened step by step."[4]

Justin's mom helped the boys come up with a name for the group. They liked the name *NSYNC because the boys all got along well together and could synchronize their voices. With Lynn Harless as one of its managers, the boys began performing around Orlando, playing gigs at restaurants, small clubs, and Pleasure Island in Disney World.

The success of the boy band Backstreet Boys helped *NSYNC get its first record contract. Boy bands were hot, and when manager Johnny Wright heard the group's harmonies he believed he could duplicate the success of the Backstreet Boys with *NSYNC. Wright signed the group and was the executive producer on the group's first album.

Signing a record contract at age fourteen made Justin feel like he was on top of the world. The prestige of being able to make a record was an immediate boost to his ego. He admitted that he let the opportunity go to his head. He felt he could do no wrong, and listened to no one but himself. "You couldn't talk to me," Justin recalled. "Nobody could tell me anything."[5]

Justin had gone from a Mouseketeer to a member of a boy band with a record contract while still a young teen. Justin felt like a star, and no one could tell him that he was anything but one. Although the contract brought him the potential for success and stardom, it would not make his life easier. Being a member of a band brought with it a great deal of work as the group prepared to make an album and promote it with a European tour.

Chapter 2

*NSYNC with His Career

Timberlake was only a young teen when he became part of *NSYNC, but he was serious about his music career. Preparing an appealing debut album was not a simple process for the group. It required a huge commitment on the part of the singers. The five group members were united in their goal of creating a top-notch recording, however, and all put in the effort it required.

Getting *NSYNC

Their manager wanted the group to build a following in Europe before releasing their record in the United States. This was a tactic that had been used successfully by other boy bands. The sugary pop sound that would be the hallmark of the group's first hits was popular in European dance clubs, so the members of *NSYNC traveled to Stockholm, Sweden, to record their first song.

Studio time was expensive so the group members were serious about making the most of their recording time. Timberlake and the others had to work both diligently and quickly to produce quality tracks on time. The song "I Want You Back" was expected to take the group four days to record, but they did it in one.

They still took the time to blend their voices on each track to bring out their best vocal qualities. On tracks such as "Sailing," a song first made popular by Christopher Cross in the 1980s, they carefully layered their voices to bring out the nuances of the

*In order to build up a fan following, *NSYNC performed in Europe before releasing their first record in the United States.*

music. "We layered that song until I don't think you could add any more harmony," Timberlake said. "We did as much with our voices as we could."[6]

The resulting album titled *NSYNC* led with "Tearin' Up My Heart" and included the popular "God Must Have Spent a Little More Time on You" and "I Want You Back."

Touring Europe

To promote the album, the group made videos and prepared to tour in Europe. They planned stops in Germany, Austria, and Switzerland. Before the tour, however, the group needed to put together a show. In addition to singing, the boys rehearsed dance routines that had them doing hip-hop dance moves in unison. Their synchronized dancing became part of the group's trademark, and its appeal. In order to get the routines perfect, they had to put in hours of practice, sometimes in uncomfortable conditions. They rehearsed in an old warehouse that was not air conditioned, and a great deal of sweat went into getting everything perfect. They were hopping around in the heat for three or four hours four times a week, and although it was uncomfortable, it gave them the strength they would need for an intense tour schedule.

Their hard work paid off when they appeared onstage. The audience appreciated not only their music, but their dancing as well. They were able to connect with the crowd and keep audiences entertained. *NSYNC was soon booked for television appearances on European channels and a sold out seventeen-city tour in Germany. Their popularity increased as they were featured in teen magazines. They quickly became so well known that the group members needed several bodyguards with them when they were in public to keep the crowds away.

The group's dance songs generated the most interest. When "I Want You Back" was released in Germany, the song quickly appeared on the music charts. It made it into the top 10 in only three weeks, becoming the fastest newcomer to hit that mark. The song stayed in the top 10 for eight weeks, the longest stay for a new act in the top 10. *NSYNC proved it was not a one-hit wonder with a popular second release, "Tearin' Up My Heart," which quickly went to Number Four. "I have hardly ever witnessed newcomers enter the German charts with such incredible, rocket-like speed,"[7] noted Thomas Stein, president of BMG Music Entertainment for the company's German-speaking territories.

Reality Check

The group's work in Germany was only the beginning. For three months Timberlake and the group toured in Europe, Mexico, South Africa, and Asia. While they gained popularity around the world, they were still relatively unknown in the United States.

Their anonymity in the United States was a reality check when they returned home. The boys were stars when they went out in public in Germany, but they were ordinary people in the

*NSYNC's success in Europe led to them being
*featured on several magazine covers like this one
from Entertainment Weekly.

United States. Timberlake and the others realized they would have to continue working if they were to become known in their own country.

The group's success in Europe also gave the members of *NSYNC time to adjust to fame. Popularity did not crush them suddenly but came to them gradually. The group members had a taste of fame, but could also retreat into an anonymous life.

Crowded field

While *NSYNC was establishing its popularity outside the United States, a number of all-male singing groups were on the radio in the United States. These boy bands included Boyz II Men, the Backstreet Boys, Hanson, and 98 Degrees. When its world tour ended, *NSYNC found itself part of a crowded field.

*As *NSYNC tried to establish themselves in the U.S. music industry other boy bands, such as The Backstreet Boys, pictured here, were dominating the pop charts.*

The competition did not discourage the group members, though. They were determined to prove that they had real musical talent. Their music followed the pop format of other boy bands, but Timberlake believed *NSYNC had more to offer. "We have no problem being compared with people—it's something that's going to happen—but I think our voices bring a real R&B feel to pop tunes,"[8] he said.

Reviewers were inclined to agree. *Billboard* writer Chuck Taylor was impressed by the quality of the group's music. He admitted that they were packaged to appeal to young audiences, but liked what he heard. He described them as "A quintet of freshly scrubbed young men whose music—surprise—is not only infectious but crisply executed and downright ambitious at times."[9] Most critics saw the group as entertaining but nothing more than a pop act with an attractive image, however. Reviewers Doug Reece and Shawnee Smith liked the song "I Want You Back," but noted that it, "Twinkles with the kind of cutie-pie candy-pop charm of Backstreet Boys."[10]

*NSYNC in the United States

Encouraged by the group's success in Europe, *NSYNC's managers and record company began promoting the group in the United States. The album *NSYNC was introduced in the United States in April 1998 and quickly became popular. The song "I Want You Back," won best dance clip and best new artist at the Billboard Music Awards and the album made it to Number 2 on the Billboard 200 list in October. Even Timberlake was surprised by the group's rapid success. "That was a little overwhelming," he says. "When I found out the album had gone to No. 2, I was jumping up and down. I didn't know what to say."[11]

With the introduction of its music on its home turf, the members of the group were now busier than ever. They began traveling around the country, doing interviews and concerts to get their name out in public. One of *NSYNC's first appearances in the United States was in a concert at Disney World. Sweat poured down their faces as the group danced and sang onstage and then introduced themselves to the crowd after the concert.

The band was relatively unknown when it played the Disney World concert, but it was soon receiving nationwide attention. In July the group was featured on a Disney Channel special that showed them riding on amusement park rides, playing at the NFL Experience at Disney's Wide World of Sports, and making music. In late October, they were chosen to be the warm-up act for entertainer Janet Jackson and also appeared on the television talk show *The View*. In addition, the group performed a Disney holiday concert special and appeared in the Walt Disney World Christmas parade. "With all of these things, everything has just taken off for these guys," said Ron Geslin, who worked for the group's record company. "There's a certain level of music production, a real mentality on their part, that I think is a cut above what some of the similar groups offer. The songs are good, the vocals are fantastic, and the production is first-class pop music."[12]

Life on the Road

Touring meant the members of *NSYNC got to ride in limousines and be greeted by screaming fans, but life on the road was not easy. The band members were busy traveling, performing, doing interviews and meeting fans, and had little time for sleep. "Right after a concert, we jump on the tour bus, still wearing our sweaty clothes, and travel for eight hours until we get to the next city," Joey Fatone told *Seventeen* magazine's Jennifer Paris. "We only get about four hours of sleep a night."

As they became more popular, *NSYNC fans devised clever ways to meet the group members. In Germany two girls pretended to faint and then jumped onstage. At the airport, another girl tried to go through the baggage security machine to get to the group. Another time, a girl hid in a hotel room closet, and a shocked Timberlake found her there.

Jennifer Paris, "*NSYNC," *Seventeen*, July 1999, p. 86.

Entertaining Concerts

Part of *NSYNC's success stemmed from the attention to detail that the group members paid to the production of their songs as well as their live performances. They layered their voices to give their recordings something special, and when they performed onstage they made sure that their shows were entertaining.

Performing fan favorites such as "Tearin' Up My Heart," "Here We Go," and "God Must Have Spent a Little More Time on You," the group members delivered an engaging and high-energy show. Whether they were shrugging their shoulders in rhythm, doing flips, or simply jumping to the beat, there was always something for their fans to watch as well as listen to.

*Becoming more popular with fans allowed *NSYNC to play larger arenas and put on more elaborate concerts.*

Big Spender

With his first big paycheck from *NSYNC, Justin bought his mom a special Christmas present. When he was young she had joked that when Justin was rich and famous he should buy her a Harley Davidson motorcycle. When his check arrived, Justin gave his mom a jewelry box with the keys to a Harley inside.

The group's first U.S. tour was more successful than they had expected. *NSYNC began its tour playing in theaters, and then moved onto larger venues such as arenas, amphitheaters and stadiums. About 1.4 million people, an average of 15,000 per show, saw their act. The group returned to some cities more than once, and received an enthusiastic reception every time.

Their shows became more elaborate as the group became more successful. Playing in larger arenas before bigger audiences allowed for more creativity. "The more success, the bigger the toys are to play with, so now it's getting really fun," Timberlake said. "Now we can use props and think more creatively. Our boundaries are becoming bigger and bigger, and we can fantasize and come up with things on a bigger scale."[13]

The group's entertaining efforts brought in crowds and impressed the critics. A concert in Nashville began with explosive fireworks and screams from the teen girls in the audience. The performance included video clips and showcased the group's musical ability as will as its ability to entertain. When they sang "Sailing" as the finale, they were suspended 30 feet above the crowd on cables. "Never let it be said the boys don't have talent," said reviewer Ray Waddell. "Not only do they showcase nonstop synchronized dance moves, they possess sizeable vocal chops and five-part harmonies to go with power-puff yet crowd-pleasing lyrics."[14]

Backlash

The group's rapid success was quickly followed by criticism of its abilities. As hard as members worked to set themselves apart, *NSYNC was one of a number of boy bands delivering similar-sounding songs. Some wondered whether the group was more style than substance, and whether it was selling itself on its members' looks and stylish production numbers rather than real talent.

Timberlake and the other group members maintained that the group had much more to offer, and that labeling *NSYNC as simply a teen pop act was unfair. They insisted that they were sincere about their music and sincere about their performances. The group wanted to deliver something their fans would enjoy.

Timberlake did not like to think of the group as a boy band or wonder how long it would all last. He simply concentrated on what he was doing and was content to deliver music that the fans enjoyed. As the youngest member of the group, he did not have a great deal of input or creative control over what they delivered, but he believed in what the group was doing. "As far as image, we're just five guys doing the music that we like to do," he said. "We don't pay too much attention to this boy band phenomenon. We just enjoy what we do and being on top and having fun. We consider ourselves a vocal group, because that's what we started off to do. We just want to entertain."[15]

Fan Adoration

*NSYNC provided more music for its fans by releasing a holiday album, *Home for Christmas*, in 1998. It contained holiday favorites such as "Home for Christmas," "The First Noel" and an *a cappella* (without accompaniment) version of "O Holy Night," but also original songs such as "Merry Christmas, Happy Holidays." The combination was appealing enough to land the album in the Billboard Top 10.

The group's teen fans did not seem interested in debating whether the group had legitimate talent or not. They wanted to buy the group's albums and learn more about them. The members

*Members of *NSYNC were so popular that fans were willing to wait outside for two days just to get their autographs.*

of *NSYNC received fifteen hundred letters a day, and the group's first album sold twelve million copies. At concerts, girls sang along with the songs and screamed for their favorite group members. Not everyone appreciated the group's combination of looks and talent as much as their young fans did, but it could not be denied that the group generated excitement. "*NSYNC are happening in a major way, and even a non-teen male can see why—they can sing, they can dance, they're cute," wrote David Wild in *Rolling Stone*. "That 'N-Syncing feeling is wholesome but not boring."[16]

No Strings

While the group members were proud of the music they were making, they soon learned that there was a business side to the entertainment industry. If they wanted to make money

Enjoying Fame

Timberlake's career kept him busy, as he recorded, toured and promoted *NSYNC. However, he also found time to enjoy fame and spend the money he was earning.

He indulged in a car collection that included three Mercedes, two Cadillac Escalades, an Audi TT, a Dodge Viper, a BMW and a Porsche. He also had five motorcycles and three jet skis. In his three-bedroom home in Orlando, he installed a pinball machine.

Timberlake was in his mid-teens when *NSYNC's popularity began to climb, and he took advantage of the perks that came with the group's success. The teen lived the rock star life, and enjoyed it. He got into clubs, went to parties and took risks. "I think I used up all my lives as a teenager," he said.

Eventually, Timberlake learned that he had to be selective in what he did. He knew there would be repercussions for the wrong choices. "You just have to remember who you are and what's going to mean the most to you down the road," he said. "Are you going to look back and say, yeah, I really had a good time? Is it going to be worth it?"

Austin Scaggs, "Justin Timberlake Revs up his Sex Machine," *Rolling Stone*, September 21, 2006, p. 50; Denise Hensley, "Lustin' for Justin," *Cosmopolitan*, November 2001, p. 80.

from their hard work, they had to pay attention to that side as well. They had been concentrating so hard on their music, concerts, and promotions that they had not looked carefully at the contract they had signed in order to become part of the music industry.

Group member Lance Bass encouraged the others to look closely at how much their management was being paid. They felt that their manager and record company were taking too large a slice of the profits. The group sought to switch record labels, and the issue went to court with members of *NSYNC claiming that Lou Pearlman, the group's first manager and head of Trans

Continental Records, had taken advantage of their trust. The release of the group's second CD was delayed by the legal wrangling as the dispute led to lawsuits and countersuits. Eventually the group moved to Jive Records, and in 2000 it released the CD *No Strings Attached.*

The title reflected *NSYNC's independence. They were now free of their first manager and felt more in control of their music. On their second CD, both Timberlake and JC Chasez got writing credits on some of the songs. When he first became part of the group, Timberlake was content to simply do what the group told him to do. As he became more comfortable with his role in the group, he sought more control over the songs it produced.

No Strings continued the group's successful streak. The 2000 release sold 2.4 million albums its first week, an industry record, and the single "Bye, Bye, Bye" climbed the charts. Fans were eager to see the entertaining group in person and broke Ticketmaster's single-day sales record for its upcoming tour when tickets went on sale in March 2000. The successful group made the cover of *Rolling Stone* magazine, an honor that both impressed and perplexed Timberlake. "When I was a kid,

*NSYNC performing during their "No Strings Attached" tour, which was so popular that it broke Ticketmaster's record for single-day ticket sales in March 2000.

I remember seeing Aerosmith on the cover of *Rolling Stone* and thinking, 'Wow, they're rock stars,'" he recalled. "I mean, they're legitimate rock stars. And when *NSYNC got our first *Rolling Stone* cover, something didn't add up for me. We were definitely not rock stars."[17]

Industry Insights

By the time *NSYNC released its second album, Timberlake had been part of the music industry long enough to realize that it was a successful pop act, but nothing more. The group members pleased audiences and worked hard to achieve a popular sound, but its niche in the music industry was confined to producing pop songs.

As time went on, Timberlake wanted something more; he was not content to simply coast along on the group's popularity. The effort he had put into the group had been a learning experience for Timberlake, and he was interested in seeing what else he could do with music and his talent.

Chapter 3

Popular Pop Star

Being a member of *NSYNC had given Timberlake the vehicle he needed to learn about the music industry and achieve his goal of becoming a performing star. He did not want to be a member of a boy band forever. While he remained a member of *NSYNC and looked forward to making a third album, he also looked for opportunities to take his talent beyond the group.

He had his sights set on furthering his career and was not afraid to try new things. He continued to write songs and tried acting as well. Timberlake had a recognizable name that would open many doors for him, and he was not afraid to take advantage of those opportunities.

Model Behavior

Timberlake's first acting job came from the same television channel he had worked for as a youngster, the Disney Channel. In 2000, at age nineteen, he made his acting debut in the movie *Model Behavior*. The movie's plot had an ordinary high school girl switching places with her look-alike, who was a model. Timberlake played the model's boyfriend.

Timberlake's role was a small one, which was fine with him. While he wanted to try acting, he readily admitted to the people at Disney that he was not a polished actor. He had done sketch comedy on *The Mickey Mouse Club* show but no serious acting. He had plenty of experience with performing, however, and showed enough promise to get the role.

Justin Timberlake and Kelly Campbell in a scene from the Disney movie **Model Behavior.**

As he did with his singing and performing, Timberlake took his work as an actor seriously. He was nervous about performing, but that made him try even harder. Although as a member of a popular boy band he had plenty of opportunities to head out at night and attend parties, he held back while he was making the movie and focused on his career rather than just having a good time with his friends. He was growing up and accepting responsibility for taking his career in another direction. "When we were shooting the movie [in Toronto], he never went out," executive producer Mike Karz said. "All he did was stay at his hotel and go to the set."[18]

The movie was not a blockbuster, but Timberlake did not mind. It was entertaining for its target audience of Disney Channel viewers. Timberlake had wanted to try something new and was happy to have the opportunity to act. "It wasn't Shakespeare," he said. "I'm not worried about what the critics say about my acting, because it's something I like to do for fun."[19]

Acting had been an interesting diversion for Timberlake, but it was not his passion. He hoped he was good enough to be considered for a role in a feature film or a television series, but music still came first.

In Love with Britney

Timberlake was in the spotlight for another nonmusical reason as well. In 1998 he had quietly begun dating pop star Britney Spears. They had worked together on *The Mickey Mouse Club* show and rekindled their friendship when she became the opening act for *NSYNC's tour. Timberlake was quickly taken by Spears, and their friendship blossomed into romance. "I was in love with her from the start," he said in an interview with *GQ* magazine. "I was infatuated with her from the moment I saw her."[20]

Although they dated, they publicly denied being a couple until summer 2000. They were spotted together at clubs in New York City and at the MTV Video Music Awards, and their desire to keep their relationship quiet only made them more sought-after by photographers. The paparazzi tracked the popular pair as they

Justin Timberlake and Britney Spears pose for photographers during an album release party in November 2001. To the public Spears and Timberlake seemed like the perfect celebrity couple.

shopped in Miami Beach and walked down Sunset Boulevard in Los Angeles.

In private, Timberlake made no secret about how he felt about Spears. He enjoyed making grand romantic gestures to show his affection. On Valentine's Day 2000, he surprised her with a special gift. During a show rehearsal, a note was delivered to Spears from Timberlake, and then a five-piece band came in and played *The Lady in My Life*.

Many considered Timberlake and Spears the ideal pop star couple. They were both good looking, entertaining performers who appealed to teens. They were living the glamorous, privileged life of stars.

For Spears and Timberlake, there were more than superficial reasons for them to be together. They had known each other before either became famous, since their days of singing duets together on *The Mickey Mouse Club*. They had spent time together as kids and knew both the fun-loving and serious sides of the other's personality. They both had been performers since they were children and were well aware of the demands of having a music career at such a young age. They had learned about the manipulative side of the music industry and knew how difficult it could be to find trustworthy people.

Spears appreciated the fact that she could be herself with Timberlake and said they were very relaxed when they were together. "When you're comfortable with someone you love, the silence is the best. And that's how me and J. are. When we're in a room together, we don't have to say anything. It's for real,"[21] she said in *Elle* magazine.

For Timberlake, his relationship with Spears was an oasis in a very busy life. When his career got too crazy, Spears was his refuge. He enjoyed having someone he could be with and talk to, someone who did not think twice about him being a celebrity. Although their busy careers and hectic schedules meant that they were often apart, they were able to set aside time to be with each other. They were successful enough to call some of the shots in their careers and go where they wanted. "We make time," Timberlake said. "We're both at the point in our careers where

Music Supporter

Once he became a successful singer, Timberlake did more than make music. He also established a foundation that helped children include music in their education.

The Justin Timberlake Foundation, formed in 2001, supported music and theater programs in schools. One of the first schools to receive money was Timberlake's old school in Memphis, E.E. Jeter Elementary. "School budgets are cut so often, and the first thing that goes is arts and theater programs," Timberlake told Debra Kaufman of *Hollywood Reporter.* "My foundation benefits these schools that have had budget cuts." Timberlake wanted to give students an opportunity he did not have when he was young. "I wouldn't be where I am today if I hadn't gone outside of school to study music, since I also attended a school with no music program," he said. "Education is important to me, and I want the kids who have the ambition to have the tools to pursue their dreams."

In 2002 Timberlake partnered with the American Music Conference, which works with a number of celebrities and organizations to help children learn about music.

Debra Kaufman, "In the Trenches," *Hollywood Reporter – International Edition.* July 24, 2001, p. 6.

we're our own bosses, and we're pretty much self-employed and have the finances to do it."[22]

Celebrity

Timberlake's financial security was due to the success enjoyed by *NSYNC. The group's tours, merchandise, and CDs were all profitable, and in 2001 the group released its fourth CD. Its title, *Celebrity*, reflected the group's popularity and in songs like the title track, group members addressed their popularity and fame. When they performed, they were greeted by screaming fans and girls carrying signs with messages for their favorite band members.

Being a celebrity was not all easy. There were safety issues to consider in addition to the heavy workload that came with touring and performing, but the group did not wallow in self-pity about the difficulties of being stars. Instead, they reveled in the success they had been working toward for years. "These boys have been thirsting for this attention since they were children, so they're entirely comfortable with their position as kings of teen pop, and they celebrate their success,"[23] noted music critic Stephen Thomas Erlewine.

Timberlake and Chasez took the lead on cowriting and coproducing most of the songs on the CD. Timberlake contributed the upbeat single "Pop" and used the album as an opportunity to learn more about songwriting. His goal was to learn more about creating music and experiment with different styles. "When we first got into this, obviously I wasn't a songwriter," he said. "But I knew that I wanted to learn it. I didn't let anybody tell me that I couldn't."[24]

On the *Celebrity* CD, *NSYNC moved away from a pure pop sound and added some rhythm and blues music to the mix. Several producers were hired to work on the CD, which included a contribution from established musician Stevie Wonder, who played harmonica on Timberlake's ballad "Something Like You." Timberlake was awed to work with such talent. "When Stevie came in to record it, that's when I knew I'd made it," Timberlake said. "I almost cried, just realizing that somebody like him is playing on a song I wrote."[25]

In addition to giving Timberlake and the others the opportunity to work with many successful people in the music industry, *Celebrity* showcased the group's versatility. The individual personalities of the group members emerged, giving the CD a personal touch that contributed to its success. The group members were by now seasoned performers and knew what their fans enjoyed. "It's the group's most varied album yet," Erlewine said, "but the emergence of Timberlake and Chasez as credible soulful singers and, yes, songwriters makes it their best album yet, and one of the best of the teen pop boom."[26]

Celebrity proved the group was not a fluke. The CD sold almost 2 million copies in its first week of release and 4.42 million copies in its first year. To Timberlake, the album represented the group's ability to be more than just a boy band. He did not worry about trying to conform to expectations or a certain sound when he wrote songs for the group, but wrote songs that he believed in. "I don't feel that *NSYNC is just a trend," he said. "All we can do is the music that we feel. I think it spoils the creativity when you have to take external things into consideration."[27]

Touring and Ending

The group supported the album with a U.S. tour that featured elaborate productions of its songs. The PopOdyssey tour featured multiple stages and used so much equipment that dozens of trucks were needed to carry it all. Set up of the set's stages, staircases, and harnesses that had the boys flying over the crowd was so elaborate that multiple versions of the stage were produced, so the process could begin in one city while they performed in another.

This elaborate tour was followed by another the following spring, although smaller in scale. The group was part of the Celebrity 2002 tour, performing with acts that included Puff Daddy, Genuine, and Smash Mouth. This tour was the group's last, however, as Timberlake and the other group members began to look at taking their careers beyond the boy band.

Timberlake still enjoyed being part of the group, but also questioned where his career was heading. As popular as the group was, he felt it had limited appeal. He had slowly but surely come to the forefront of the group and felt it was time to see what he could do on his own. Thanks to his relationship with Spears, he was by far the best known of the group's members. He was also a talented musician and performer whose success stemmed from his ability as well as his desire. Name recognition and talent gave Timberlake a strong head start as he struck out on his own.

Justin Timberlake performing during the Celebrity Tour 2002. This would be the last tour that *NSYNC would participate in together.

Timberlake was not the only group member who felt it was time to try something new. Lance Bass applied to go on a shuttle launch with the Russian Space Agency, Joey Fatone appeared in the movie *My Big Fat Greek Wedding*, and JC Chasez recorded a solo album of his own. The group had enjoyed enormous success, but its members wanted to explore other options for their careers. It did not officially break up, but they did not record another album together.

Timberlake wanted to make music that showed his individuality. As he learned more about the music industry, he broadened his musical tastes and abilities. He realized he needed to break away from the pop sound that had made *NSYNC so popular. "I think that whole time [with *NSYNC] I was living in some small shape of oblivion," Timberlake said. "I thought, 'They're just putting that teen-pop label on us because they don't understand. 'I look back now and realize that that's exactly what it was."[28]

Relationship Trouble

Timberlake was pursuing his own in his music career, and was soon on his own in other ways as well. His relationship with Spears ran into trouble in 2002. They found it more difficult to find time to be together and Timberlake suspected Spears was cheating on him, although this was never confirmed. Their relationship ended after nearly four years together.

Timberlake was genuinely hurt when their relationship ended. He could not even say the word "breakup" in an interview, stating that it was too painful to say aloud. He admitted that he cried himself to sleep.

The pair had a public relationship, and their breakup was newsworthy as well. There was much speculation that the two would get back together, but there was also talk of Britney dating others. That hurt Timberlake even more. "I feel like I'm in the middle of a soap opera," he said. "I honestly know what it's like to have a broken heart now."[29]

Timberlake also reflected on the good times he and Spears shared, and the good things she had brought to his life. He said

Laying Down the Law

After breaking up with Britney Spears, Justin Timberlake outlined some rules for making a relationship work. They included love, communication, and trust. Love is the basis for everything, he explained to Michelle Tauber of *People* magazine in 2002. "You start to have a chemistry with someone, and then you fall in love."

Communication was important, he added. "So many times when you date, you don't really communicate," he said. "You think it's okay to not say how you feel because the whole butterflies-in-your-stomach vibe that you keep getting every time you see the person is cute. Then they do something and you kind of let it go because you think it's a cute thing. That's a big no-no."

Finally, he noted that a relationship won't work without trust. "If you didn't communicate with that person from the very beginning, they can't trust you. If you communicated to that person everything you were feeling and you said exactly how you felt, and you woke up every morning doing what you thought was right and that person did not trust you, then there's nothing you can do at that point and you have to walk away."

Michelle Tauber, et al, "Justin Timberlake," *People*, June 24, 2002, p. 58.

he still loved Spears, and always would. "I can't sit here and say that she's been a dark part of my life," he said. "She's been a big sunshine in my life. I've learned so many things."[30]

New Outlook

After the breakup, Timberlake became focused on deciding what to do with his future. He did not want to be rushing from one concert to the next but desired time to reflect on what he wanted to do with his music. He realized how busy he had been in recent

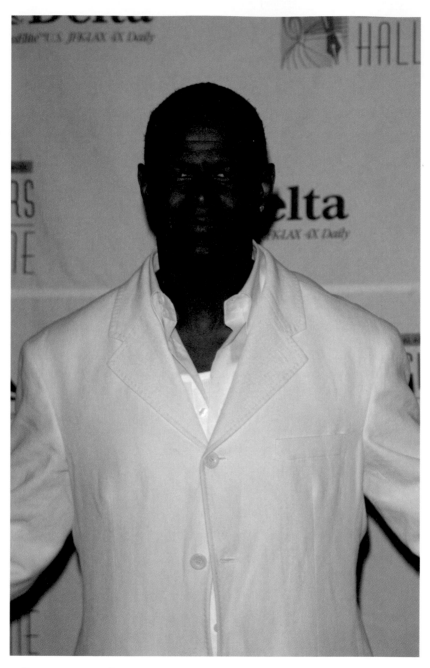

After going solo with his career and breaking up with Britney Spears, Timberlake had time to hang out with friends like R&B singer Brian McKnight.

years and wanted to carefully consider where he was going. He said. "I want to enjoy the simple things. I want to take three days off when I want to, not when it's on my calendar. I want to go run in the park with my sweats on because I can. That's where I'm at right now."[31]

Once he scaled back, Timberlake found plenty of ways to fill his time. He hung around with friends such as R&B singer Brian McKnight, challenging him in Xbox and PlayStation games or driving their sports cars. In 2002, Timberlake again made headlines for his personal life. There were rumors that the 21-year-old was dating Janet Jackson, who was 36 at the time, and then Alyssa Milano, the star of the television show *Charmed*.

In addition to taking his personal life in a new direction, Timberlake soon took his career on a different route as well. The entertainer now knew enough about the music industry to take his career where he wanted it go to and in 2002, the same year his relationship with Britney ended and *NSYNC went on hiatus, he began recording a solo album. He had earned fame and fortune and the celebrity lifestyle as a member of *NSYNC. Now he wanted something his music had not yet given him in his career—respect.

Chapter 4

Justified Reputation

Timberlake took a chance by leaving a successful group to record a solo album. There was no guarantee that the success he had earned as a member of a group would carry over into his solo career. The singer had learned a great deal while with the group, however, about songwriting, album production, and performing. He was eager to use what he had learned to develop his own style. In addition to his drive and talent, Timberlake had another factor in his favor. Thanks to his relationship with Spears and the media attention they received, his name was more recognizable than that of most boy band members.

He worked at creating a sound that would earn him respect as a musician and singer. The album's title showed his desire to prove that he was worthy of being admired for something other than a member of a popular boy band. He called his first solo album *Justified*.

Rich Music

On *Justified*, Timberlake wanted to be known for more complex music than the pop songs *NSYNC had produced. While *NSYNC's music had been enjoyable to teens and preteens, it was not something other artists respected. To develop a richer and more personal sound, Timberlake added elements of hip-hop, funk, and rhythm and blues styles to his music.

Timbaland (left) was just one of the producers who worked with Timberlake to create the unique sound found on Justified.

For Timberlake, this was a natural expression of his varied musical interests. He explained that he had eclectic tastes, stemming in part from his roots. Some listeners might be surprised by his new sound, but to him it was simply an outgrowth of who he was and the musician he was becoming. "In a group, people don't get to see everybody's individual personalities," he said, "they just see the unit. But now they see there is this side of me and it's surprising. But I grew up in Memphis where blues was invented."[32]

Timberlake knew better than to try to create these new sounds on his own. With *NSYNC he had worked with a number of record producers and knew that each brought his own strengths into the studio. For his solo debut, he tapped into his contacts in the music industry. He got help from producers such as Timbaland, Chad Hugo, and Pharrell Williams of the Neptunes. These producers helped Timberlake create the unique, appealing, and danceable sound that was his goal.

Flaming Lips

Timberlake showed that he was not afraid to do something unusual when he jammed with the British group The Flaming Lips in 2003. While in England, he met the group in the hallway at the British television network BBC. He mentioned that he had the group's records, and singer Wayne Coyne asked if Timberlake would like to play with them.

Timberlake agreed to join the band for "Yoshimi Battles the Pink Robots," and he played bass on the song for the British television show *Top of the Pops*. The group wore costumes onstage, so Timberlake put on a dolphin suit. In the final minute, he took off the head of the disguise, to the surprise and delight of the audience. "Girls in the audience screamed," Coyne told Shirley Halperin of *Rolling Stone*.

Shirley Halperin, "Psychedelic Timberlake," *Rolling Stone*, March 6, 2003, p. 23.

It took only six weeks to write and record *Justified*. Throughout that time, Timberlake was both directing the album's sound and learning from the people with whom he was working. He appreciated the feedback the producers gave him. "To make an album, it takes both those personalities," he said, "somebody who's dictating what they definitely want and somebody to be the coach, who can sit on the sidelines and say, 'Yeah, I think that's it.'"[33]

Independence

A number of the songs on *Justified* reflected Timberlake's independence, both as a musical artist and in his personal life. He was on his own after seven years as part of a popular group. In addition, at the time he was recording the album he was still stinging from his breakup with Spears.

The songs on the album reflected Timberlake's perspective on life at the time. He was anxious about being on his own and suffering from a broken heart. Writing songs for the album became therapeutic as he dealt with many changes. About half the songs on the album were autobiographical, he said, and the other half a fantasy.

The personal nature of the songs on *Justified* showed how much he believed in his new musical venture. Timberlake realized that he could be heavily criticized for his music. However, he needed to try something new if he was to grow as a musician. "If I feel it in my gut, I just leap," he said. "That's my philosophy with everything. If you fall down, you figure it out for the next time."[34]

A Hit

Timberlake's gut feeling about his career move was correct. When his solo debut album was released in November 2002, it was a resounding success. Critics loved it, with *Rolling Stone* calling it a "bona-fide killer dance record."[35] It eventually sold more than 4 million copies.

When he listened to the music he and the others had created on *Justified*, Timberlake realized he had achieved exactly what he had set out to do. He had developed a distinct sound for himself and had proven himself as an artist in his own right. He said the music on *Justified* was ten times better than anything *NSYNC had ever done, and he even gained admiration from Lou Pearlman, who had formed *NSYNC. Admiring Timberlake's vocal and musical ability, Pearlman called him "the whole package," adding, "He can go all the way."[36]

The album was the highlight of Timberlake's year and he was proud of his accomplishment. "I love to be in the studio writing music, and this album is all me," he said. "I am happy with it."[37]

"Cry Me a River" Controversy

Timberlake's first solo album was not without controversy. The song "Cry Me a River" was said to be about his breakup with Spears, and the song's video contained a Britney look-alike. It looked as if Timberlake was getting back at Spears with the video and song as it implied that Spears cheated on him, and that he was the one who was wronged and hurt by their breakup.

Timberlake downplayed the controversy of the video, saying that it actually made him look like the one who had done something wrong. The video showed him retaliating by being with another woman, and making sure the Spears character knew about it. "What is all the fuss about?" he said. "If anybody is the bad guy in the video, it's me."[38]

When questioned about Spears, Timberlake said he had loved Spears from the moment they met and he had no bad feelings toward her. They still spoke, he said, and maintained a civil, friendly relationship. "People think that when people break up they're enemies, but I grew up with this girl," he said. "So we're going to be friends. We have a lot of history. It's as simple as that."[39]

At the same time, he admitted that he had been stung by Spears' actions after their breakup. He felt that Spears had opportunities

Beauty and Brains

Music is not the only thing for which Timberlake is admired. In 2003 he was named to *People* magazine's list of the sexiest men. "He's got a huge heart—that's what makes him sexy," said his friend Sharon Osbourne. "Usually you get guys who are gorgeous and a bit of a dummy. He is so talented yet so nice and smart."

People, "No. 5 Justin Timberlake," December 12, 2003, p. 84.

to speak up for him but did not. He was hurt by this, and dealt with his feelings via the song and video.

New Image

The controversy over the "Cry Me a River" video helped Timberlake's evolving image. With *NSYNC he had been a clean-cut member of a group that focused on a core audience of young teens. The group had been wholesome and safe, and as a solo artist Timberlake was ready to be more daring.

With *Justified*, Timberlake showed an edgier side, not only with his music but with his personality as well. He was still sensitive, as evidenced by the pain he felt over his breakup with Spears, but the way he dealt with his pain in the video suggested a darker side.

Timberlake reinforced the new version of himself by appearing shirtless on the cover of *Rolling Stone*. It was not a planned move, and he was at first unsure of how it would be accepted. The reaction he received told him that it had been the right decision. "Chicks started coming up to me, and I was like, 'Yeah!', as if I had masterminded this whole sex-appeal thing on purpose,"[40] he says.

Solo Performer

Timberlake had to invent a new image as a performer as well. When he toured and made television appearances to promote his new album, he was onstage without the other four singers he had been used to performing with for seven years. He had been in the spotlight in the past, but not for the entire show. Now the success or failure of a performance was all on his shoulders.

Timberlake made his first solo appearance on television on the MTV Video Music Awards in August 2002. Emerging out of a giant boom box, he sang "Like I Love You" and performed dance moves reminiscent of Michael Jackson, a performer he had admired for years. Some people criticized his performance because he dressed so much like Jackson, with gloves and a cocked hat, but Timberlake was making a statement. Like Jackson, who left the Jackson 5 to break out on his own, Timberlake was leaving the group behind and was coming out as a solo act. It was the beginning of a new era for Timberlake.

Timberlake toured the following year to promote his new album, heading to Europe in 2003 for his first solo concerts. He was anxious about performing alone, but once the audience

Justin Timberlake amazed the audience with his first solo performance at the MTV Music Awards in 2002.

began responding to his music, the performance went fine. "The outcome has been way more than I could have every hoped for," he said. "And they sing every song."[41]

As he had with the production of his album, Timberlake had a great deal of control over the show and had a clear vision of what he wanted it to be like. He used medleys to keep the music flowing continuously and included heavy doses of dancing. "I hate going to a show and feeling like it's a recital," he said. "I'd rather it feel continuous, like a club. You go to a club and the DJ doesn't stop, he just spins from one song to the next."[42]

Timberlake's touring schedule was demanding, and it was not easy being out of the United States. Not every show went well. He did a summer concert in Toronto in 2003 that was met with a horrible reception. The benefit concert included The Rolling Stones, AC/DC, the Guess Who, and Rush, and Timberlake wondered if the fans at the concert who were there to see the hard rock acts would appreciate his music. He quickly found that they did not. He did three songs before being pelted with water bottles thrown by the crowd.

The show in Toronto, however, was the exception to the rule. Most crowds adored him. Timberlake was happy to be admired for what he could do, not just because he was a star. "It's a liberating thing to walk onstage and see people your age and up," he said. "And they're not screaming just because you're standing there, they're screaming because you did something to impress them. They don't put your poster on their wall—they just like your record."[43]

Back Home

That summer he toured in the United States as well. Joining him was former Mouseketeer Christina Aguilera, whose voice he admired and who had also recently been at the top of the pop music charts. They did not perform together in the concert, but each took their turn with solo performances. Timberlake's show was impressive; he brought a fourteen-piece band with him on the road, climbed on a crane during the performance, and used

Justin Timberlake performing in Oakland, California, in 2003 during his tour with Christina Aguilera.

video images to entertain the crowd. His singing was effortlessly on pitch and his dancing was reminiscent of Michael Jackson, with reviewer Carly Carioli noting that, "He looked as weightless as a moonwalk"[44] when he performed in Boston.

The tour gave him something else he didn't often have: privacy. When he did not have to be onstage he could go to his dressing room and prepare for the performance, alone. "I crave alone time," he said.

> I think sometimes you get these people who become obsessed with the four-letter word fame. To me, it doesn't exist. There's nothing that says that any of us entertainers are a pinky nail in length more important than the guy who builds the streets in New York City. I mean, he's doing a lot more than I am for society.[45]

Timberlake did not become reclusive, however. He needed some time to himself but remained sociable. After the show was over for the night, he did not stop performing. He would often do an after-show performance at a small club. He and his band would make music, without scenery, props, or choreographed dances. This helped him grow musically and gain more credibility as a performer and musician.

In addition to bringing him respect, *Justified* brought Timberlake awards. In 2003, he won the VMA award for Best Dance Video for *Rock Your Body*. He also won two Grammy awards and three MTV Video Music Awards for the album. His music brought him compliments from his peers in the music industry. When he was applauded by rap artists 50 Cent and Eminem when he received the award for Best Male Video at the Video Music Awards, he saw it as an accomplishment. He was surprised and relieved that they respected him and his music.

Transformed

When he made *Justified*, Timberlake wanted to prove to himself and the music industry that he was more than just a singer in a pop band who was getting by on good looks and the marketing efforts of his manager. He created his own sound, learning from respected music producers such as Timbaland how to bring creativity into his work. The result was more successful than he had dreamed it would be. Timberlake himself was amazed at how one album had transformed his image and career. "The whole year was weird for me," he said. "Before that, I was just a boy in a group. There was a lot of naiveté involved, and we didn't really understand the weight of the phenomenon."[46]

Once he made the cover of *Rolling Stone* as a solo act, he felt like people were actually listening to his music. He had moved far beyond doing simply what others told him to do and performing songs he was expected to sing. He was being innovative with the production of his music and was creating something new for people to enjoy. The album was a huge moment in his career, as he had fought for respect and won it. Many now viewed him as a credible singer, musician, and songwriter. "I didn't want to be that 'guy from the boy band,'" Timberlake said. "I didn't want to

Justin Timberlake, the winner of several MTV Video Music Awards in 2003, felt his success was especially satisfying because of the difficulties he experienced the previous year.

be that guy who is just, like, famous for being famous. I didn't want to be the guy who dates girls in the tabloids. That's why the album was such a big deal for me. I had to fight harder for my respect, my credibility."[47]

His success was especially liberating because of the difficult times he had endured in 2002, the year of his breakup with Spears. He was surprised and relieved to have so many good things come his way the following year. "Last year was the most tortuous year of my life," he said in 2003. "And this year, it's as if some higher power was like, 'All right, you passed that test, now here you go, here you go, here you go.'"[48]

Chapter 5

More Than Music

While he was proving himself as a singer and songwriter, Timberlake did not confine his talent to the music industry. As the *Justified* tour wound down he looked to use his talent—and his popular name—in other ways. He had proven himself a capable musician and was free to try new things, including reviving his fledgling acting career.

After making his solo album, Timberlake was so busy touring and making appearances to promote it that he did not have the time or energy to really think about what he would do as a follow-up to *Justified*. When the topic of his future came up, the veteran performer said he considered doing some work behind the scenes for other performers or even retiring by age thirty. However, he admitted that he did not have any firm plans for the next year of his life.

Acting Surprise

There was no shortage of work for Timberlake in the entertainment industry. He rekindled his television career with an appearance on *Saturday Night Live* in 2003. A perfectionist at whatever he did, he prepared thoroughly for his time onstage. Although he was the show's guest host, he did not rely on the show's regulars to carry his performance. He wanted to contribute and have the audience enjoy his appearance.

Timberlake was comfortable in front of a live audience and was used to sketch comedy from his days on the *Mickey Mouse Club*. He surprised many viewers as well as those in the

Besides music, Justin Timberlake enjoys playing basketball, and even took part in an advertising campaign for the NBA.

audience with his adept turn at humor. His acting, comedy, and timing were impressive as he confidently dressed like entertainer Jessica Simpson and impersonated actor Ashton Kutcher. He did not ignore the fact that singing was what he was known for, however, and performed "Cry Me a River," "Rock Your Body" and "Senorita."

Timberlake also appeared in television commercials. He made cameo appearances in commercials for McDonald's, which had hired him to write a hip-hop jingle for its "I'm Lovin' It" advertising campaign. Although music was his profession, he also loved playing basketball, so it seemed only natural that he take part in an advertising campaign for the NBA that featured celebrities who "Can't Get Enough" of basketball. He was scheduled to do some work as a special television correspondent for the NBA, appearing on ABC Sports, but that job floundered as Timberlake realized he was more of a fan than an analyst.

Timberlake showed that he could take a joke when he became the subject of a prank on the first episode of *Punk'd*, a show produced by Kutcher that put celebrities in awkward situations and waited for their reaction. Kutcher had people impersonating IRS agents go to Timberlake's home and convince him that he owed hundreds of thousands of dollars in back taxes, so his cars and other possessions were being repossessed. The prank brought Timberlake to the verge of tears as even his guitar was packed up. Just as he was about to break down, Kutcher walked in and the prank was revealed. A relieved Timberlake took it in stride, but warned Kutcher that "This means war!"[49] and got back at him with his impersonation of Kutcher on *Saturday Night Live*.

New Relationship

As Timberlake took some time away from music, he deepened his relationship with a new girlfriend. He began dating actress Cameron Diaz in 2003, after they met at the Nickelodeon Kids' Choice Awards. Diaz was a Los Angeles native, a model, and an actress who had appeared in movies such as *The Mask, There's Something About Mary* and *Charlie's Angels*. She was also the voice

Despite their nine-year age difference, Cameron Diaz and Justin Timberlake began a three-year relationship after meeting at the 2003 Nickelodeon Kids' Choice Awards.

of Princess Fiona in the animated film *Shrek*. Known for her beauty, Diaz also has a humorous side and once won the belching contest at the Kids' Choice Awards.

Diaz was older than Timberlake, 31 to his 22, but despite their nine-year age difference the pair had much in common. Both were interested in the outdoors and sports. They vacationed in Hawaii, where they surfed and enjoyed relaxing on the beach.

The relationship between the two good-looking celebrities did not go unnoticed by the press. They had to deal with interest from the tabloid press whenever they were together, and their vacation was interrupted by the many photographers looking to get a picture of the couple. By now, however, Timberlake was a veteran at dealing with fame. He convinced photographers to keep them a certain distance away from him and Diaz. He had just left a celebrity relationship that had been well chronicled by the press and did what he could to control the intrusion this time.

He had professional as well as personal reasons for wanting to keep the photos at a manageable level. He did not want the bulk of his recognition to come from a celebrity relationship. He had worked too hard on his music for that. He preferred to enjoy his time with Diaz as part of a couple, not as another way to get his picture into the paper and boost his career.

He and Diaz could not stop speculation about the state of their connection. As their relationship progressed, there were constant rumors that they had broken up, and also rumors that they were engaged. Although neither was ready to commit to marriage, Timberlake said his relationship with Diaz was more of an adult relationship, while the relationship he had with Spears had been like a high school one.

Super Fiasco

While Timberlake and Diaz tried to keep their relationship as private as possible, his public appearance with a former girlfriend was anything but hush-hush. Timberlake appeared with Janet Jackson during the Super Bowl halftime show in February 2004. The show was filled with other stars including Kid Rock, Sean "P. Diddy" Combs, and Nelly, and the pair was looking for something to set their duet apart. To make it memorable, they planned to do a "reveal" at the end of their number by pulling off a piece of her wardrobe.

At first they considered using a long skirt, but Jackson found the skirt too difficult to dance in. They then decided to rig her bodice so a red bra would be revealed when Timberlake pulled

*The 2004 Super Bowl halftime show by Janet Jackson
and Justin Timberlake was one of the most talked about
performances in recent history.*

it downward. Their plan worked too well. At the end of the
number, Timberlake grabbed Jackson's bodice and ripped downward. It was supposed to reveal a red bra, but instead showed
Jackson's breast.

The resulting uproar over the incident led to cries of indecency
and later resulted in a fine for the network. There were questions
about whether or not the incident was planned, and Timberlake
apologized for the indecent scene on the Grammy Awards show
the next week. After he won the award for male pop vocal, for
"Cry Me a River" he said. "I know it's been a rough week on

Photo Woes

Timberlake was often followed by photographers but tried not to let their presence bother him. There were times when he just got tired of being followed, however. At one point he slapped a photographer who Timberlake felt had crossed the line. After meeting with the district attorney, he realized violence was not the answer. "We live in an interesting time where everybody and everything is completely accessible," he explained to *Rolling Stone* writer Austin Scaggs. "And I love what I do, but I also love my life and my privacy."

Austin Scaggs, "Justin Timberlake Revs up his Sex Machine," *Rolling Stone*, September 21, 2006, p. 50.

everybody … What occurred was unintentional, completely regrettable, and I apologize if you guys were offended."[50] The audience supported him with a round of applause.

Some wondered if Timberlake got off too easily, while Jackson bore the brunt of the negative publicity for the incident. There was criticism for him not supporting her more strongly. Timberlake admitted that Jackson was the one who carried most of the burden in the uproar that followed. The incident certainly did not hurt his popularity. He continued to try new projects in his time away from the studio and tour and remained a singer who was in demand.

Crossover Appeal

Timberlake kept out of the public eye after the Super Bowl, but did not abandon music completely. Always interested in new musical styles, he showed that he could appeal to fans of many different types of music by appearing on Snoop Dogg's hit song *Signs*. He also showed up on the album *Monkey Business* by the Black Eyed Peas, a group he had also worked with on their *Elephunk* CD. When he attended one of the Peas concerts in Los Angeles, he hopped on stage and joined in with the group, as his girlfriend Cameron Diaz snapped pictures with her cell phone.

Timberlake showed that he does not have to always be the star of the show. He was content to make music and be in the background as he collaborated with other artists. His time with *NSYNC had taught him the value of working as part of a group. Working alongside a rap artist or hip-hop group helped Timberlake's reputation as well, as it cast him as a musician who appealed to a broad audience.

One group he was no longer working with, however, was *NSYNC. In 2004, Timberlake officially ended his participation in the five-member pop group. He met up with his former singing partners in Miami to sing the National Anthem at a charity event, and the other members of the group expected to soon set a date to begin recording their next album. However, Timberlake indicated that he was not interested. He had worked hard to establish his own sound and an individual direction with his career, and his focus now was on his solo career, not another album with a pop group.

Edison

Timberlake did not yet have the energy to return to the recording studio or go on tour, but he did not abandon his career. He went in a new direction, away from music and toward movies with an appearance in the movie *Edison*. He played an investigative journalist in the thriller starring Morgan Freeman and Kevin Spacey.

The movie was filmed in Vancouver, Canada, during summer 2004, and the experience allowed him to expand on the acting career he had begun with his work *Saturday Night Live*. "*SNL* was like a playground," he said. "And the reason I got into film is because I needed something inspiring, but more intimate, that I didn't have to do in front of 180,000 people every night."[51]

Justin Timberlake's role in the film Edison *allowed him to work with veteran actors, such as Morgan Freeman, and to expand on his previous acting experience.*

Making *Edison* was much more involved than sketch comedy, however. The full-length film meant going on location to make the movie and spending days on the set. In addition to learning his lines and working on his acting, the celebrity also had to deal with fans who camped out on the street outside his rented home. He dealt with them by bringing along his own security staff while on location. The experience was not all work for Timberlake, who visited clubs in the evening and went to restaurants with Diaz when she visited him on the set.

Clothing line

When Timberlake took a break from recording in 2005, he dabbled in fashion. He had a well-known name and a solid image that could be used effectively to market things besides music. With his friend Trace Ayala, he started the William Rast clothing line. It was named after Justin's grandfather, William, and Ayala's grandfather, whose last name was Rast.

Timberlake had a large supporting role in the movie, and was billed third following the film's two stars. His second foray into acting did not receive a great deal of attention, however, as the film received mediocre reviews and went straight to video.

Much-Needed Rest

Timberlake's acting venture also gave him the opportunity to rest his singing voice. He had developed throat nodules (benign growths on the vocal cords) and had them successfully removed in an operation in the spring of 2005. Full recovery required that he take time off and use his voice as little as possible.

Timberlake used his time away from music to expand his horizons and take a much-needed rest. In addition to dabbling in acting on *Saturday Night Live* and in movies, he spent some time relaxing and living life at a regular pace. "That was amazing for me," he said. "Just the little things, like sitting home on the weekend or making a Sunday tee time."[52]

In addition to playing golf, Timberlake snowboarded and surfed. Feeling rejuvenated and inspired, he was now ready to return to singing and songwriting and prepared to head back to the recording studio.

Chapter 6

Commanding Performer

Timberlake was primed to make music after his break. Although he had received respect from *Justified* and enjoyed successful CD sales, he did not try to recreate the sound of his first solo album. Once again he was prepared to try something new. He took chances with *Justified*, and was ready to do the same with his second solo effort.

As he had realized with *Justified*, Timberlake knew he could not create an album on his own. He brought in producers such as Timbaland to boost his creativity. Once again, he met with success as *FutureSex/LoveSounds* appealed to both music critics and average listeners. He did not let his other interests fade, however, as he continued acting and expanding his career horizons.

Something Different

As Timberlake prepared to make his new album, he felt he could create something that was better than the music he heard being played on the radio. He wanted to bring a new sound to the airwaves. "I knew that I needed something new," he said. "I wanted to take more of a chance—experiment."[53]

He began recording the new album in December 2005, spending a few weeks in the studio and then taking a few weeks off. He was by now very familiar with all aspects of creating music, from writing songs to the technology that went into production, and was heavily involved the entire process. The popular record

Justin Timberlake and Timbaland performing one of the songs off of Timberlake's second solo CD during the 2006 MTV Video Music Awards.

producer and rapper Timbaland had helped out on Timberlake's previous album with tracks such as "Cry Me a River," and also contributed to the music and vocals on Timberlake's new CD. He was amazed by how everyone in the studio worked together and contributed. "Everybody's creativity was at a peak, and everybody was just throwing ideas into the pot,"[54] he said.

Timberlake came up with the songs' lyrics, verses, bridges, and choruses while they were in the studio. His ability to put a song together without writing down the words impressed those he worked with. "Everybody knows he's talented, but this dude wrote that whole album without touching a pen or paper," said producer Nate "Danja" Hills. "I've heard stories about Jay-Z or Biggie doing that, but I've never heard of a singer doing that. I think it's some sort of superpower."[55]

Timberlake enjoyed the creative process, but although he had been enormously successful with his previous album, he was not

Realizing his Faults

Timberlake is a perfectionist who knows how he wants things to work, but realizes that this sometimes rubs others the wrong way. When Timberlake has an idea he wants to pursue, he does so with an intensity that requires some personal space. He also has a temper, stemming from his penchant to be a perfectionist.

Timberlake admits that the way he has treated other people is not perfect. "I'm always genuinely nice to people, but there have been times when I've gotten so invested in my seclusion that I've pushed people away," he confessed to Austin Scaggs of *Rolling Stone*. "but I've realized that the way I act has an effect on people."

The singer also impresses people with his ability to take charge, however. "It's as if Justin had been born 26 years ago to deliver music to the world," said Timbaland, who worked with Timberlake on the CD *FutureSex/LoveSounds*. "There are those who follow and those who lead. Justin is a leader, setting the bar for what's expected of others."

Austin Scaggs, "Justin Timberlake Revs up his Sex Machine," *Rolling Stone*, September 21, 2006, p. 50; Timbaland, "Justin Timberlake," *Time South Pacific*, May 14, 2007, p. 83.

confident about how this one would be received. When he made *Justified*, he had little to lose and everything to gain from being creative and innovative as he worked to build a reputation. Now, people expected more from him and he worried about living up to those expectations. He sometimes had nightmares about whether his music would be accepted.

Well Received

Timberlake need not have worried. *FutureSex/LoveSounds* was considered by many to be edgy, innovative, and danceable and as good, or better, than its predecessor. Chuck Arnold of

People magazine called it an "exhilarating follow-up," adding, "Timberlake delivers highlight after highlight, from the spacey, falsetto-sweetened hip-hop of 'My Love' to the haunting, gospel-infused strains of 'Losing My Way.'"[56]

Timberlake had made a record that could appeal to fans of many styles of music. Innovative hits such as "SexyBack" and "What Goes Around" received a great deal of radio airplay. The album was also popular in nightclubs, as its songs were made for dancing. But while Timberlake had created the music with dance clubs in mind, he wanted to offer something for other listeners as well. "There's no doubt that it's a club record," he said, "but there's a rock sensibility about it."[57]

Timberlake was reaching out to varied audiences with his album, from hip-hop fans to listeners who liked dance music. He was rewarded for his efforts with two Grammys for *FutureSex/LoveSounds*. At the 2006 awards, he and Timbaland won for Best Dance Recording for "Sexy Back" and Best Rap/Sung Collaboration for "My Love," which featured rapper T.I. He also performed on the show, playing and singing "What Goes Around."

Refining his Image

Timberlake was happy for the success of *FutureSex/LoveSounds* but said in some ways he was really not like the image that came through on the album. He certainly did not feel like he was as cool as a person he sang about in "SexyBack." "I write about what I know, but I also write about things that are just fantasies in my head," he said. "I don't really think I brought sexy back. It just seemed like something catchy to say. I don't really think of myself that way. It's just fun. It's like acting, because you create a character in your mind, and you run with it."[58]

Timberlake had a broad and varied fan base. He kept in touch with kids by appearing on shows such as Nickelodeon's Kids Choice Awards and being a good sport when he got covered with green slime. His dance music was popular with young adults. His songs received airplay on Top 40 stations and he appealed to hip-hop fans as well because of his collaborations with Timbaland and other rappers.

On Stage

Timberlake's image continued to evolve on stage as well. *Justified* had earned him respect and had proved that he had the talent to become a solo artist. With his second solo effort, he took another step. With shows at clubs such as the House of Blues, he moved even further away from his boy band past and began entrenching himself in the music industry as an artist with staying power. In his club concerts, Timberlake impressed the audience by concentrating on music rather than dancing or flashy lights. He led a band, played keyboard and guitar, and sang vocals. Everything

After the release of his second solo CD, Timberlake's live performances concentrated more on music and less on dancing and flashy lights.

Secret Recipe

Timberlake opened a New York restaurant in 2007 that reminded him of home. As reported by Michelle Tan in *People* magazine, The restaurant, Southern Hospitality, which he opened with friends Trace Ayala and Eytan Sugerman, features barbecue ribs, corn bread and fried chicken. The restaurant also offers pulled pork collard greens, green beans and macaroni and cheese.

The restaurant's décor is meant to remind Timberlake of places in Tennessee. There is memorabilia from Johnny Cash, Hank Williams, Jerry Lee Lewis, and Elvis on the wall, and a golf video game for patrons to play.

The restaurant's food reminds Timberlake of the dishes his grandmother made, but he also keeps a stash of her home-made goods at home. She sends him jars of blueberry jam and squash relish that he loves so much he does not share them. "I tell everybody to stay away from the mason jars in my cupboard," he said. "Do not touch!"

Michelle Tan, "He's Bringing Gravy Back," *People*, August 6, 2007, p. 70.

he did was "imbued with a passion and professionalism that make his musicianship seem like far more than a token pull for credibility,"[59] Miller wrote. He also showed that he had wide appeal by including an appearance by the hip-hop group Three 6 Mafia and producer and singer Timbaland in his show.

In addition to playing small clubs, Timberlake also performed before much larger audiences as he toured to promote his new album. Appearing at Madison Square Garden in 2007 before a sold-out audience, he delivered a performance that highlighted his musical talent as well as his ability as a performer. He provided funky beats, played keyboards, and even did some comedy with *Saturday Night Live's* Andy Samberg. He danced with elaborate choreography and used video screens, lighting effects and a

Eytan Sugarman (left), Justin Timberlake, and Trace Ayala opened the New York restaurant Southern Hospitality in 2007.

central stage to add interest to his performance. His music was "as if the funk of the future had finally arrived," wrote Gavin Edwards of *Rolling Stone*. "Timberlake commanded the crowd's attention just by striding around the stage that was unquestionably his."[60]

Timberlake was just as comfortable before a sold-out crowd in Boston that year, appearing before an audience that included a heavy dose of screaming female fans. He gave a high-energy performance, reviewer Lauren Carter noted, as he sang vocals, played multiple instruments and handled the show's choreography with effortlessly. The show paid homage to his years with *NSYNC with the song "Gone" and also his *Justified* album with

"Cry Me a River." Timbaland joined him on tour, giving them a chance to do their duet "SexyBack" for audiences.

The shows weren't perfect. Some criticized the long intermission that had Timbaland spinning records like a DJ, while others thought the screens and stages were distracting. In general, however, respect came Timberlake's way, both from audiences and fellow entertainers. He was now respected as a musician, not just a singer, dancer or songwriter. His improvisational attitude toward music impressed others, including his former boy bandmates. "The kid has stepped out," said JC Chasez, former member of*NSYNC. "He's grown by leaps and bounds. He's a Jedi."[61]

End of a Relationship

Timberlake's career was going smoothly with the success of *FutureSex/Love Sounds*, but his personal life had hit some rough spots. He and Diaz ended their relationship in 2006. After three years together, they publicly announced that they were no longer a couple.

Some speculated that their relationship ended because she was ready for marriage and children and he was not. Others said that she got upset when he hired Scarlett Johansson for his video "What Goes Around," even though Diaz thought of Johansson as a rival actress. Timberlake and Diaz did not release much information, however. They had not been outgoing about their relationship when they were together, and were just as discreet when they broke up. They released a statement that said that, although it had been their practice not to comment on their relationship, they felt compelled to do so because of speculation and inaccurate stories. "We have, in fact, ended our romantic relationship, and have done so mutually and as friends, with continued love and respect for one another."[62]

Timberlake was as quiet about his post-Diaz relationships as he had been about his relationship with Diaz. After splitting with Diaz, he was linked to Johansson, as well as actresses Alyssa Milano and Jessica Biel. He admitted to talk show host Oprah Winfrey that he had a girlfriend, whom many speculated was

After his breakup with Cameron Diaz, it was speculated that Justin Timberlake was involved in a relationship with actress Jessica Biel.

Biel. Although he and Biel had been spotted together acting like they were a couple, he still declined to name his girlfriend. He did say that, "I get pretty romantic around her,"[63] noting that he sings to his girlfriend and keeps in touch by Webcam when they're apart.

Movie Maker

Timberlake did not let the ups and downs of his personal life affect his career, and he continued to diversify his work with movies. Despite the disappointing outcome of *Edison*, he fed his interest in acting with a number of supporting roles. "Justin could have had a starring role," said director Craig Brewer, who directed Timberlake in *Black Snake Moan*. "But he's aware that audiences are cynical about music stars crossing over into acting."[64]

In *Black Snake Moan*, released in spring 2007, Timberlake played an anxiety-ridden National Guardsman. The film starred Samuel L. Jackson and Christina Ricci, and Brewer felt Timberlake could bring the depth needed for his smaller role as a troubled young man. "When I approached him for it I said, 'It's a vulnerable role, and I really want you to tap into something.' He understood that,"[65] said Brewer.

The movie centered mainly around Jackson, who played an ex-blues musician, and Ricci, who played a young woman whose life is heading downhill. The movie was criticized for its plot, although Timberlake emerged unscathed. "Black Snake Moan will indeed have you moaning, 'Please, make it stop!'" wrote reviewer Lisa Rozen. "The idea seems to be that these two damaged people can eventually help each other to heal. This is hooey of the highest order."[66]

Branching Out

Timberlake's next film fared better, as he again expanded his acting range and moved even further away from the good-boy pop star image that had made him a star. In *Alpha Dog*, he played a

Business Venture

Timberlake entered another avenue of the recording industry in summer 2007 when he became chairman and CEO of Tennman Records. He launched the Los Angeles-based business with Interscope Records, and one of his jobs was to recruit new talent for the label.

"I've run the gamut on things I can do for myself [as an artist]," he explained to *Entertainment Weekly* reporter Margeaux Watson. "I feel inspired to give someone else a chance to have what I've been lucky enough to have."

The first singer signed to the label was Esmee Denters, a Dutch singer who gained popularity by posting videos of her performances on YouTube. Through his company, he also planned to do songwriting and production for established groups such as Duran Duran.

Finding new talent like Denters and working with other artists made his work interesting, Timberlake said. He doubted that he would ever really stop working. "It's gonna have to take something pretty apocalyptic," he said. "I don't know that I'll ever retire."

Margeaux Watson, "Justin Timberlake [Mogul in the Making]," *Entertainment Weekly*, June 29, 2007, p. 88.

tough guy covered with tattoos. His reputation as a singer made one of his costars unsure of him as an actor, but once filming started he earned her respect. "I really wasn't sure about him because he's a singer," said Amanda Seyfried, who acted with him in *Alpha Dog*. "But he blows me away."[67]

In the movie, Timberlake played Frankie, a thug who was assigned the job of guarding a young man who was kidnapped by a drug dealer. Critics found the movie itself to be average, but were impressed by Timberlake's performance. "This is a fine, fierce dramatic performance, alive in the eyes, in the gestures that reveal a scared kid under Frankie's bravado," wrote Peter Travers

*Justin Timberlake earned respect as an actor for the tough-guy role he played in the 2007 film **Alpha Dog**.*

in *Rolling Stone*. "You watch Timberlake in this movie and you want to see him take on bigger risks."[68]

Timberlake showed that he was not afraid to try varied roles. He did voice work for the animated movie *Shrek the Third*, voicing the character of a young king. In the satire *Southland Tales*, he played a solider opposite Sarah Michelle Geller. He also showed that he could act with a comic touch with a well-received skit performance with Andy Samberg on *Saturday Night Live*.

Bad reviews of some of Timberlake's movies did not seem to hurt his image. He was not the star, so the success or failure of the film was not on his shoulders. Some said his success at acting was helped by his experience in working in an ensemble. He eased into acting more quickly than a solo star would have.

"When a diva is doing a stage performance, they are in control, and the focal is on them," said James Robert Parish, author of the book *Hollywood Songsters*. "When they share scenes, few can interact and volley back and forth. He came out of a group, and they learned how to do a performance, to make a little production out of each song."[69]

Looking Ahead

Timberlake certainly is good at collaborating onscreen, on television and in the music studio. While he enjoys making music, and has been doing so for fifteen years, he sees himself gradually easing out of performing and into other aspects of the entertainment industry. "Ten years from now, I don't want to be jumping around onstage,"[70] he said.

Timberlake is again ready to take himself out of the spotlight for a while, although he plans to remain busy. He envisions more movie work in his future, and says that before he does any more music he has to reenergize. "I can't just pump out 20 more songs and expect them all to be 'What Goes Around,'"[71] he said.

He has not left the music industry completely, however. He did some work for other singers, writing for Macy Gray, collaborating on a country song for Reba McEntire and working with 50 Cent on his album *Curtis*. He explained that he had a varied interest in musical styles, and wanted to explore them all. "I want to write country music because that's where I grew up—Tennessee," he said. "Soul music … I want to be involved in hop-hop. And sometimes I feel the only way to really express all those different sides, even just for myself, is through different people."[72]

Making an album and promoting it took two years, he said, and he cannot imagine continuing to do that for a lifetime.

He sees himself living in Los Angeles and Tennessee, and having another home in Europe. Performing and music are a very fulfilling part of his life, but Timberlake realizes there is more to life than work. He plans to reappear on the entertainment scene, but only after he has recharged. "Just float around—not too shabby, right?" he said. "The dream is to be able to have a schedule I've had like the last five years, to put out a record and tour, then take a little break, maybe do some films. But I don't want to work this hard forever."[73]

Chapter 1: This Kid Has Rhythm

1. Austin Scaggs, "Justin Timberlake Revs up his Sex Machine," *Rolling Stone*, September 21, 2006, p. 50.
2. Jeremy Helligar, et al, "Boy Power," *People*, February 8, 1999, p. 93.
3. Anthony Breznican, "Timberlake Turns away from Spotlight," *USA Today*, May 1, 2007, p. 01d.
4. Chuck Taylor, "Following Its Soulful Instincts, RCS's *NSYNC Set to Break Away from Boy-Group Brigade," *Billboard*, April 18, 1998, p. 72.
5. Scaggs, "Justin Timberlake Revs up His Sex Machine." *Rolling Stone*, September 21, 2006, p. 50.

Chapter 2: *NSYNC with His Career

6. Taylor, "Following Its Soulful Instincts, RCS's 'NSync Set to Break away from Boy-Group Brigade," *Billboard*, April 18, 1998, p. 72
7. Wolfgang Spahr, "Ariola act is *NSYNC with German fans," *Billboard*, June 21, 1997, p. 47.
8. Taylor, "Following Its Soulful Instincts, RCS's 'NSync Set to Break away from Boy-Group Brigade," *Billboard*, April 18, 1998, p. 72.
9. Taylor, "Following Its Soulful Instincts, RCS's 'NSync Set to Break away from Boy-Group Brigade," *Billboard*, April 18, 1998, p. 72.
10. Douge Reece and Shawnee Smith, "New & Noteworthy," *Billboard*, Jan. 17, 1998, p. 66.
11. Chuck Taylor, "*NSYNC Spends Its 'Time' Evolving Into More Than Just A Teen Pop Sensation," *Billboard*, November 7, 1999, p. 104.
12. Taylor, "*NSYNC Spends Its 'Time' Evolving Into More Than Just A Teen Pop Sensation, *Billboard*, November 7, 1999, p. 104.

13. Taylor, "*NSYNC Spends Its 'Time' Evolving Into More Than Just A Teen Pop Sensation, *Billboard*, November 7, 1999, p. 104.

14. Ray Waddell, "In Concert: *NSYNC Nashville Arena, March 30," *Amusement Business*, April 12, 1999, p. 9.

15. Taylor, "*NSYNC Spends Its 'Time' Evolving Into More Than Just A Teen Pop Sensation," *Billboard*, November 7, 1999, p. 104.

16. David Wild, "NSync," *Rolling Stone*, November 12, 1998, p. 59.

17. Jenny Eliscu, "Justin Grows Up," *Rolling Stone*, May 18, 2006, p. 210.

Chapter 3: Popular Pop Star

18. Dave Karger, "And Justin for All," *Entertainment Weekly*, March 10, 2000, p. 57.

19. Jason Lynch, "Talking with…Justin Timberlake," *People*, March 13, 2000, p. 32.

20. ABC News, "Justin on Britney: 'In Love From the Start,' www.abcnews.go.com/print?id=2217905.

21. Dan Jewel, "Pop's Puppy Lovers," *People*, November 27, 2000, p. 85.

22. Denise Hensley, "Lustin' for Justin," *Cosmopolitan*, November 2001, p. 80.

23. Stephen Thomas Erlewine, "Celebrity Album Review," *All Music Guide*, www.bilboard.com/bbcom/discography/index. jsp?pid=261075&aid=483805.

24. Rebecca Wallwork, "Justin Timberlake," *Interview*, Feb. 2003, p. 48.

25. Denise Hensley, "Lustin' for Justin," *Cosmopolitan*, November 2001, p. 80.

26. Stephen Thomas Erlewine, "Celebrity Album Review," *All Music Guide*, www.bilboard.com/bbcom/discography/index. jsp?pid=261075&aid=483805.

27. Denise Hensley, "Lustin' for Justin," *Cosmopolitan*, November 2001, p. 80

28. Jenny Eliscu, "The New King of Pop," *Rolling Stone*, December 25, 2003, p. 44.

29. Michelle Tauber, et al, "Justin Timberlake," *People*, June 24, 2002, p. 58.
30. Tauber, et al, "Justin Timberlake," *People*, June 24, 2002, p. 58.
31. Tauber, et al, "Justin Timberlake," *People*, June 24, 2002, p. 58.

Chapter 4: *Justified* Reputation

32. *Newsweek*, "Justin Timberlake," November 11, 2002, p. 78.
33. Rebecca Wallwork, "Justin Timberlake," *Interview*, Feb. 2003, p. 48.
34. Tauber, et al, "Justin Timberlake," *People*, June 24, 2002, p. 58.
35. Ben Ratliff, "Justin Timberlake," *Rolling Stone*, November 28, 2002, p. 86.
36. Susan Horsburgh, et al, "Justin Time," *People*, November 11, 2002, p. 73.
37. Margo Whitmire, "Timberlake's Appeal 'Justified' by Solo Success," *Billboard*, December 7, 2002, p. 22.
38. Eliscu, "The New King of Pop," *Rolling Stone*, December 25, 2003, p. 44.
39. *Newsweek*, "Justin Timberlake," November 11, 2002, p. 78.
40. Jenny Eliscu, "Justin Grows Up," *Rolling Stone*, May 18, 2006, p. 210.
41. *Rolling Stone*, "Justin," June 26, 2003, p. 50.
42. *Rolling Stone*, "Justin," June 26, 2003, p. 50.
43. Jenny Eliscu, "The New King of Pop," *Rolling Stone*, December 12, 2003, p. 44.
44. Carly Carioli, "The Justin & Christina variety show," *The Boston Phoenix*, Aug. 15, 2003, http://bostonphoenix.com/boston/music/top/documents/03084976.asp.
45. *Rolling Stone*, "Justin," June 26, 2003, p. 50.
46. Eliscu, "Justin Grows Up," *Rolling Stone*, May 18, 2006, p. 210.
47. Associated Press, "Justin on Britney: 'In Love From the Start,'" http://abcnews.go.com/pring?id=2217905.
48. Eliscu, "The New King of Pop," *Rolling Stone*, December 12, 2003, p. 44.

Chapter 5: More Than Music

49. TV.com, "Punk'd Episode Guide- Punk'd Season Episodes," http://www.tv.com/punkd/show/17441/episode.html.
50. Ken Barnes, "Music, not scandal, is the star," *USA Today*, February 9, 2004, p. 01d.
51. Scaggs, "Justin Timberlake Revs up his Sex Machine," *Rolling Stone*, September 21, 2006, p. 50.
52. Scaggs, "Justin Timberlake Revs up his Sex Machine," *Rolling Stone*, September 21, 2006, p. 50.

Chapter 6: Commanding Performer

53. Scaggs, "Justin Timberlake Revs up his Sex Machine," *Rolling Stone*, September 21, 2006, p. 50.
54. Brian Hiatt, "Pop's New Hitmaker," *Rolling Stone*, October 5, 2006, p. 18.
55. Scaggs, "Justin Timberlake Revs up his Sex Machine," *Rolling Stone*, September 21, 2006, p. 50.
56. Chuck Arnold, "Justin Timberlake," *People*, September 18, 2006, p. 47.
57. Scaggs, "Justin Timberlake Revs up his Sex Machine," *Rolling Stone*, September 21, 2006, p. 50.
58. Anthony Breznican, "Timberlake turns away from the spotlight," *USA Today*, May 1, 2007, p. 01d.
59. Jeff Miller, "Justin Timberlake," *Daily Variety Gotham*, August 14, 2006, p. 15.
60. Gavin Edwards, "Justin Timberlake," *Rolling Stone*, March 8, 2007, p. 98.
61. Scaggs, "Justin Timberlake Revs up his Sex Machine," *Rolling Stone*, September 21, 2006, p. 50.
62. *People*, "Justin Timberlake and Cameron Diaz Break Up," *People*, January 11, 2007, www.people.com/people/article/0,,1142562,00.html.
63. Digital Spy, "Timberlake admits relationship to Oprah," September 20, 2007, www.digitalspy.co.uk/showbiz/a76049/timberlake-admits-relationship-to-oprah.html.
64. Tim Stack, "Justified Acting Career?," *Entertainment Weekly*, April 28, 2006, p. 20.

65. Stack, "Justified Acting Career?," *Entertainment Weekly*, April 28, 2006, p. 20.
66. Leah Rozen, "Black Snake Moan," *People*, March 12, 2007, p. 34.
67. Oliva Abel, et al, "Justin Through the Years," *People*, July 18, 2005, p. 26.
68. Peter Travers, "Alpha Dog," *Rolling Stone*, January 25, 2007, p. 80.
69. Breznican, "Timberlake turns away from spotlight," *USA Today*, May 1, 2007, p. 01d.
70. Scaggs, "Justin Timberlake Revs up his Sex Machine," *Rolling Stone*, September 21, 2006, p. 50.
71. Breznican, "Timberlake turns away from spotlight," *USA Today*, May 1, 2007, p. 01d.
72. Breznican, "Timberlake turns away from spotlight," *USA Today*, May 1, 2007, p. 01d.
73. Scaggs, "Justin Timberlake Revs up his Sex Machine," *Rolling Stone*, September 21, 2006, p. 50.

1981

Justin Randall Timberlake is born on January 31 in Memphis, Tennessee.

1992

Timberlake makes his television debut as a contestant on *Star Search* but does not win.

1993

Timberlake is asked to join the cast of *The Mickey Mouse Club*.

1995

The musical group *NSYNC is formed, with Timberlake, JC Chasez, Joey Fatone, Chris Kirkpatrick, and Lance Bass.

1996

*NSYNC's first album is released in Europe and the group tours in Europe and Asia as well as South Africa and Mexico.

1998

*NSYNC's debut album is released in the United States. Its holiday album, *Home for Christmas*, is released in November.

2000

*NSYNC's third album, *No Strings Attached*, is released and sets a record for selling 2.4 million copies in the first week of its release. Timberlake appears in the Disney Channel movie *Model Behavior*.

2001

*NSYNC's fourth album, *Celebrity*, is released and Timberlake contributes to the songwriting and production of a number of the album's tracks.

2002

Timberlake ends a 3½-year relationship with Britney Spears. In late fall, his first solo album, *Justified*, is released to critical acclaim.

2004

Timberlake's appearance in the Super Bowl halftime show with Janet Jackson causes a stir when he rips away part of her costume and reveals her breast. Timberlake wins two Grammy Awards, for "Cry Me a River" and *Justified*.

2006

FutureSex/LoveSounds, Timberlake's second solo album, is released and is well received.

2007

Timberlake wins two Grammy Awards, for "Sexy Back" and "My Love." He stars in the film *Alpha Dog* and receives solid reviews for his acting.

For More Information

Books

Martin Roach, *Justin Timberlake: The Unofficial Book*. London: Virgin Books, 2003. This photo-filled book aimed at his fans tracks Timberlake's career from his days with *The Mickey Mouse Club* to his success with *NSYNC and as a solo artist.

Sean Smith, *Justin: The Unauthorized Biography*. London: Simon & Schuster, 2004. This easy read looks at Timberlake's music career and explores his personal relationships.

Kimberly Walsh. Just Justin: Get with *NSYNC's Total Babe! Scholastic: New York, 2000. This book from the Backstage Pass series has information about Timberlake's early years with *NSYNC.

Periodicals

Ann Powers, "Justin and Britney: A Tale of Two Lives and Careers," *Los Angeles Times*, September 13, 2007, www.lateims.com/entertainment/news/music/la-et-britneyweb14sep 14,0,4041875.

Web Sites

Justin Timberlake, www.justintimberlake.com. Timberlake's Web site has videos as well as information on his music and tours.

Internet Movie Database, (www.imdb.com/name/nm0005493/maindetails). This Web site offers photos, a brief biography of Justin Timberlake and an updated list of his acting work.

People (www.people.com). Celebrity news is featured on this Web site. A search for Timberlake brings up information about the star.

Entertainment Weekly (www.ew.com). News about Timberlake and other stars is the focus of this Web site.

Terri Dougherty has written more than 50 books for children. She lives in Appleton, Wisconsin, with her husband, Denis, and their three children, Kyle, Rachel, and Emily. She is amazed by Justin Timberlake's musical talent and dancing ability.